CROCODILES & ALLIGATORS

SEYMOUR SIMON

HarperCollins*Publishers*

People have known about and feared crocodiles and alligators for centuries. Early peoples made up all kinds of stories about these giant reptiles with their long tails. Fables of fire-breathing dragons and giant serpents that ate humans were probably based upon crocodiles and alligators. Yet stranger than all these tall tales is the true story of crocodiles and alligators.

There's even a strange story behind the word "crocodiles," because these animals got their name from early Greek travelers who first saw the animals on the banks of the Nile River in Egypt. The crocodiles reminded them of a small lizard called *krokodilos* that lived back in Greece. The name means "pebble worm," because the lizard was long and thin and hid among the rocks. So the giant crocodiles got their name from a tiny lizard.

Alligators got their name from Spanish explorers in Florida who called them *el lagarto*, which means "the lizard." The only other animal very closely related to crocodiles and alligators is called a *gharial*, shown here. The word comes from India, where gharials live. The word means long, thin jar, but in the gharial's case it is the jaws that are long and thin.

Despite an alligator's or a crocodile's fearsome looks, watching one in a zoo may seem as exciting as watching grass grow. Alligators and crocodiles lie nearly motionless for a long part of each day. You might think that they are dull and uninteresting. But nothing could be further from the truth.

Alligators or crocodiles basking in the sun are all eyes and ears on the alert for prey. Lying quietly helps them to surprise prey animals as they launch an explosive attack. The giant reptiles are also soaking up warmth from the sun so they don't have to use their own energy.

Alligators and crocodiles spend most of their time in water, where they may attack any animal that gets too close, from a fish to a person. Crocodiles and alligators use their powerful jaws to capture their prey, because they cannot chew their food. If the prey is too large to swallow in one gulp, they tear it apart. Sometimes they drag large prey below the surface, where it drowns. Then they use their strong tails to spin around in the water, ripping at the body of the prey. Even though crocodiles and alligators spend a lot of time just lying in the sun, they're anything but boring when they spring into action!

Alligators and crocodiles, along with caimans (relatives of the alligators) and the gharial, are the living members of a larger animal group called crocodilians. Crocodilians are reptiles with long bodies and tails, short legs, and sharp teeth in powerful jaws. They have been around since the age of the dinosaurs, 100 million years ago. The crocodilians are one of the longest-running reptile shows in the world. As far as weight is concerned, the largest living reptile is a crocodilian.

Reptiles are land dwellers (although many can swim), lay eggs, and breathe with lungs. Their thick, scaly skin helps protect them from enemies and prevents their body fluids from drying out in the air. Reptiles are cold-blooded, which means that they do not have an internal source of body heat, as mammals do. So crocodilians depend for their warmth upon the heat they get from the sun.

There are twenty-three different species of crocodilians: fourteen kinds of crocodiles, six kinds of caimans, two kinds of alligators, and one gharial. All these crocodilians live in tropical and subtropical areas or the warmer, moist regions of the Temperate Zone. Alligators are the major kind of crocodilian that lives in the United States.

Crocodilians and dinosaurs are close relatives. Both belong to an animal group called archosaurs, which means "ruling reptiles." There were many more dinosaur species than crocodilians, and the dinosaurs also lived in many different kinds of climates.

The crocodilians just kept living in warm, wet places around the world and always looked about the same. Then, 65 million years ago, all the dinosaurs became extinct. With the dinosaurs gone, the crocodilians became the biggest and smartest reptiles left in the world. No one knows why the dinosaurs disappeared but some of the crocodilians thrived.

Even large crocodilians were usually smaller than the biggest dinosaurs, but there were some exceptions. Some of the crocodilians that lived in the age of the dinosaurs werc even longer than *Tyrannosaurus rex*, one of the largest meat-eating dinosaurs. *Phobosuchus*, which means "terrible crocodile," may have been 50 feet long, as long as a large trailer truck. The head of this terrible crocodile was 6 feet in length, and the mouth contained 4-inch teeth.

How can you tell the difference between crocodiles, alligators, and caimans? One easy-to-see difference is that alligators and caimans have a wide, rounded snout that looks like the letter U, shown here, top. Crocodiles usually have a much more pointed snout that looks like the handle of a baseball bat, shown here, bottom.

Alligator and caiman jaws are good for crushing hard-shelled animals such as turtles. Crocodile jaws are not quite as powerful when it comes to crushing, but are more useful in catching different kinds of foods such as fish.

Another difference between alligators and caimans and crocodiles is the way their teeth are positioned in their jaws. In alligators and caimans the jaws are very wide, and the upper jaw completely overlaps the lower one. So the teeth of the lower jaw are almost completely hidden when the alligator closes its mouth. Also, the large fourth tooth of the lower jaw fits into a special socket in the upper jaw.

In crocodiles, the teeth in the lower jaw can be seen even when the mouth is closed. The large fourth tooth also fits outside the upper jaw when the mouth is closed.

Other differences cannot be spotted as easily. Small sensory pits cover most of a crocodile's body, but these pits are found only around the jaws of alligators. Some people think that crocodiles are more aggressive than alligators, but that's not true in every species.

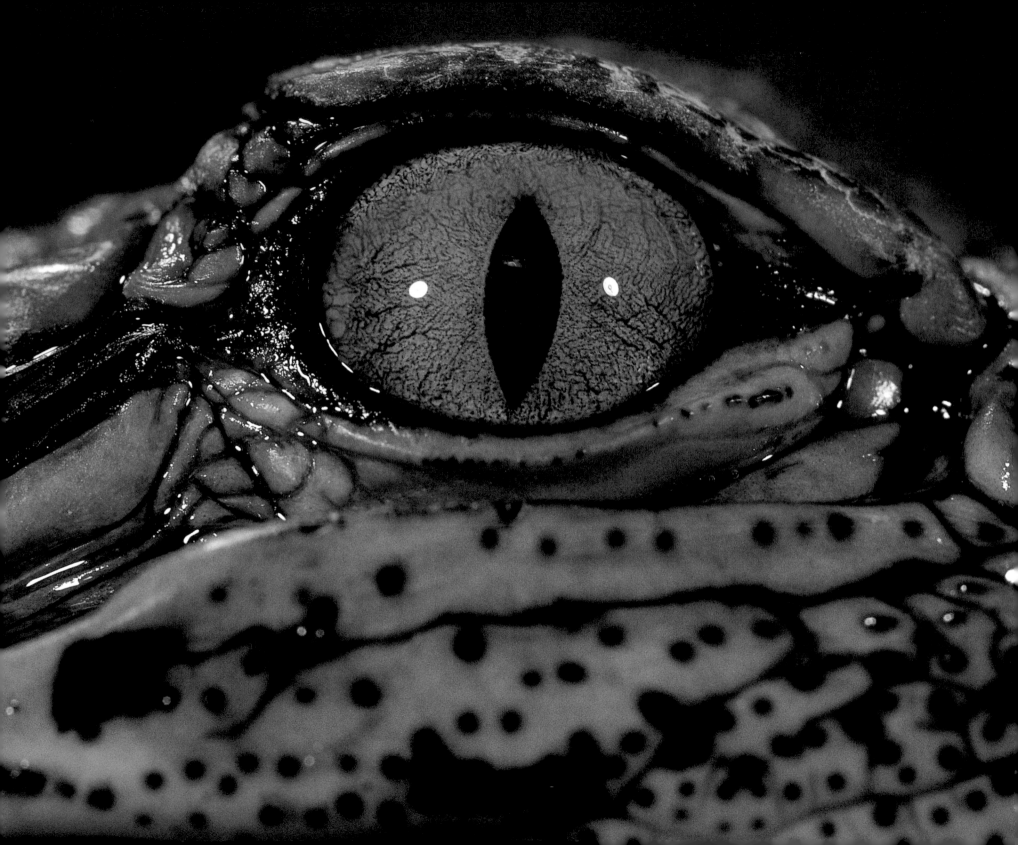

Crocodiles, alligators, and gharials share many features that allow them to live in water and on land. They all have long, powerful tails and streamlined bodies that allow them to swim powerfully and easily. They have legs and feet for walking on land. Crocodilians are very strong animals, and their bodies are covered by a tough, scaly hide. As a result, adult crocodilians have few natural enemies that are strong enough to harm them — except, of course, humans.

Crocodilians' legs are short and not as strong as their tails. They have five long toes on each front foot, which allows them to move firmly on the ground. The back feet, with their four toes, are used like rudders for steering in the water. The neck, body, and tail of a crocodile are strong and muscular. Bony plates, called osteoderms, protect the body like shields.

Crocodilian jaws have huge muscles that snap tight. But the muscles that open the jaws are weaker. Some people can hold the jaws of a crocodilian shut with their hands! That's certainly not something for you to try.

Crocodilians have eyes, but they do not cry "crocodile tears." The phrase refers to a person who is insincere and tries to gain sympathy where none is deserved by pretending to cry. Crocodilians have no tear ducts, which is probably what people were thinking of when they made up the phrase. But they do have a third eyelid that sweeps across the eye to clean and protect it, and that lid may assist in underwater vision.

The biggest crocodilian (and also the biggest reptile) in the world is the Australian saltwater crocodile. In the 1960s in Australia there were reports of 20-foot-long saltwater crocodiles. That was before many of them were killed for their hides. Some hunters recall shooting crocodiles that measured more than 26 feet long.

Do larger ones exist? We may never know. There are "big fish" stories that people tell of crocodiles that are more than 30 feet long, but no one has ever actually measured a crocodile that size.

Many other crocodiles are almost as big as the saltwater crocodile, including the South American Orinoco crocodile and the Indian mugger crocodile. The Indian gharial is reported to reach over 19 feet long. These are all the biggest sizes reported. Most crocodilians, such as the Nile crocodile shown here, grow to about 10 to 12 feet. When they hatch, crocodilians are a bit less than a foot long. The babies grow rapidly and triple their length in two years. Their growth begins to slow down after that.

Crocodiles grow for as long as they live, but just how long *do* they live? One of the oldest crocodiles ever known died recently in a zoo in Russia at an age of more than 110 years. Gomek, a crocodile that died at an alligator farm in Florida in 1997, was around 70 to 90 years old and about 19 feet long. He had been captured as an adult in Papua New Guinea, and his age at that time was unknown.

The crocodilian species that grow the oldest appear to be the ones that are the largest. The saltwater and the Nile crocodiles are thought to live around 70 years on average, and some may be more than 100 years old. Other kinds of crocodilians do not live nearly as long. Alligators and caimans may live for only 30 to 40 years. It seems to be clear that the stories of crocodilians living for hundreds of years are simply not true.

We have no sure way of telling the age of a crocodilian, though measuring growth rings in bones and teeth gives an approximate age. An animal's habitat may affect how long it lives and how fast it grows. Animals that are raised in zoos or on farms probably live to different ages than animals living in the wild. The stress of being caged up, incorrect diet, disease—all these factors can cause an animal to die in captivity. On the other hand, there are no natural predators to harm captive animals. Perhaps the average age of captive animals is higher than in the wild, but it is also possible that the very oldest crocodiles live in the wild in places where conditions are excellent for their growth and survival.

Crocodilians are wonderful hunters in the water. They can submerge and remain underwater for many minutes at a time — for more than an hour if necessary. Large crocodilians may attack almost any animal that comes near them in the water. They are so strong that most animals are helpless against them. Once they grab hold of prey with their powerful jaws and pull it under the water, very few animals can ever escape.

Crocodilians are also very good at swimming right up to their prey without being seen. Their eyes and nostrils are located at the tops of their heads, so they can breathe and look around above the surface although only the tops of their heads show. That's why people learn to be careful when they go near a crocodile-infested river or stream.

Crocodilians eat fish, small mammals, turtles, and birds. Some larger crocodilians, such as the Nile crocodile, may attack larger animals such as antelopes and even lions or tigers. But a crocodile that attacks a lion or a tiger or a hippopotamus may be biting off more than it can chew. A hippopotamus is strong enough to defend itself and even kill a crocodile.

A Nile crocodile will eat almost anything it catches, but not a small bird called an Egyptian plover. The plover walks right into a crocodile's mouth and picks food from between its teeth without the crocodile clamping down!

It's clear that crocodilians are most dangerous when in the water, but can a crocodilian catch a human running away on land? Some stories tell of crocodilians running as fast as 25 miles per hour, much faster than a human. But the truth is that a person can usually outrun a crocodilian on land. Here's why:

There are three main ways a crocodilian moves on land. The "belly crawl" is a slow push that a crocodilian uses to slide over slippery ground. The crocodilian uses its legs to push itself along. Humans could easily outrun a crocodilian doing the belly crawl.

The next way is the "high walk," in which a crocodilian gets up on its legs and moves fast, more like a mammal than a reptile. By using a combination of the belly crawl and the high walk, shown here, the crocodilian moves its body from side to side in a swimming motion and can move its legs very rapidly. This is how a crocodilian usually moves when it is heading toward water. Crocodilians can travel about 9–10 miles per hour for a short period of time, which is a little slower than a human can run for a long time.

The fastest method is called "galloping." In this strange way of moving, the crocodilian bounds forward almost like a dog, using its hind legs to power the rest of its body forward. This style of running is seen in only a few smaller species and allows the animal to leap over low objects on its way to the water. By galloping, a small crocodilian can reach a speed of 11–12 miles per hour, just about as fast as many humans. But the crocodilian can maintain this speed and movement for only a few steps.

Snakes, turtles, and most other reptiles generally lay their eggs and leave them to hatch on their own. But crocodilian mothers defend the nest and care for their young for several months afterward. It's fortunate that they do, because crocodilian eggs and babies are tasty morsels of food for many other animals. Without their mothers' protection, most of the eggs and babies could be eaten.

Crocodilian eggs have to be incubated in a nest for several months at temperatures around 88°F. in order to hatch. The temperatures for the first several weeks determine whether the embryo will develop into a male or a female. Females usually develop at lower temperatures, and males develop at slightly higher temperatures.

Crocodiles and alligators build different kinds of nests. Most crocodiles dig a hole in the ground and lay as many as sixty eggs in two or three layers. The eggs are covered with sand to keep them warm. But if the ground gets too hot, the mother may splash water on the nest to keep it cool.

Alligators build their nests out of leaves, branches, and mud above the ground. The mother shapes them into a mound about 6 feet wide and 3 feet high. She scoops out a hole in the center and lays as many as seventy eggs in the hole, then covers them up. As the leaves and branches decay, they give off heat and help keep the eggs warm.

A mother Nile crocodile keeps a close watch on her nest from the shade of a nearby bush or tree. During the two or three months that the eggs take to hatch, the mother is almost always on guard, neither wandering away nor feeding. She will growl and charge at any animals that come too close to the nest. The father stays nearby too, but he does not approach the nest, because even he will be attacked by the protective mother.

The eggs swell inside the muddy nest. Then the shells crack into pieces, but the leathery internal lining remains. Each hatchling uses its pointy egg tooth to rip through the egg case and tries to crawl out. But the babies are still not free. The outside of the nest has been baked in the sun and is as hard as cement. As the young begin to bark and cry loudly, the mother hastens over and rips through the hardened nest.

The mother rolls the eggs on the ground to help the young escape. Then she opens her gigantic mouth, and the young crawl in. When her mouth is full, the mother carries the hatchlings to the water and releases them.

The hatchlings spend their first few weeks protected by their watchful parents. After the baby crocodiles use up the food stored in their bodies, they begin to eat water bugs, frogs, and other small animals. The babies stay with their parents for as long as three months before setting out on their own.

The American alligator lives in swamps and marshes through the southeastern United States, from Florida north to the Carolinas and west to Oklahoma and Texas. At one time adult males over 15 feet long were often found in the wild, but nowadays alligators larger than 12 feet are rarely seen. Females usually reach lengths of less than 9 feet. Adult alligators seem to be either long and thin or short and stocky.

In the past the American alligator, and crocodilians all over the world, were thought to be threats to humans and livestock. Efforts were made to eliminate them for this reason. Crocodilians were also hunted for meat and for their hides, which were turned into leather for shoes, belts, and handbags. Illegal hunting and smuggling of the hides continued even after protection laws were enacted in the 1960s. By 1972 all the crocodilians in the world were either endangered, threatened, or declining in number.

But with additional laws to protect the alligator and other crocodilians, populations of the animals are improving. Bringing crocodilians back from the edge of extinction is the primary job of the Crocodile Specialist Group, an international conservation network. In the past twenty-five years the Crocodile Specialist Group has nurtured sixteen of the twenty-three species of crocodilians back to increased population levels. This is a truly remarkable record.

Alligators and crocodiles play an important role in their natural surroundings. In many ways they help the environment to remain healthy. For example, throughout the Everglades swamps of south Florida, alligators thrash out the grasses and dig in the mud to create pools called "gator holes," where water collects. When the flow of water dries up in winter, the Everglades become vast stretches of brown saw grass and cracked mudflats.

But in and around the gator holes life goes on, even during the dry season. Catfish, garfish, frogs, and other water animals swim in the ponds. Fish-eating birds such as anhinga and herons search for food in the shallows. Deer feed on the grasses that surround the pond. The alligator shapes the land for itself and also provides good living conditions for other animals until the rains come in the spring.

Like many other wild animals, crocodilians are chased away by people building houses, roads, bridges, and dams. But with proper understanding of what to do and a willingness to share the natural resources of the land, people of goodwill can prevent crocodilians from becoming as extinct as the dinosaurs.

To Jeremy Scott Simon, with love from Grandpa

Special thanks to Dr. Louis J. Guillette, Jr., Ph.D., of the University of Florida, for his expert advice.

Photo credits

Jacket, 13 (bottom), 18, 32, © Tom McHugh/Photo Researchers, Inc.; p. 1, © Arthur Morris/Visuals Unlimited; pp. 2–3, © Leonard Lee Rue III/Photo Researchers, Inc.; p. 5, © 1990 by Alok Kavan/Photo Researchers, Inc.; pp. 6, 13 (top), © Tom & Pat Leeson/Photo Researchers, Inc.; p. 9, © Bill Bachman/Photo Researchers, Inc.; p. 10, © Alan D. Carey/Photo Researchers, Inc.; p. 14, © Joe McDonald/Visuals Unlimited; p. 17, © 1972 by M. P. Kahl/Photo Researchers, Inc.; p. 21, © 1992 by Fritz Pölking/Dembinsky Photo Association; p. 22, © Cyril Toker/National Audubon Society; p. 25, © Dr. Robert H. Potts, Jr./Photo Researchers, Inc.; p. 26, © Nigel J. Dennis/Photo Researchers, Inc.; p. 27, © Adam Jones/Photo Researchers, Inc.; p. 29, © J. H. Robinson/Photo Researchers, Inc.; p. 30, © Jeff Lepore/Photo Researchers, Inc.

Library of Congress Cataloging-in-Publication Data
Simon, Seymour.
    Crocodiles and alligators / Seymour Simon.
        p.   cm.
    Summary: Describes the physical characteristics and behavior of various members of the family of animals known as the crocodilians.
    ISBN 0-06-027473-5 — ISBN 0-06-027474-3 (lib. bdg.)
    ISBN 0-06-443829-5 (pbk.)
    1. Crocodilians—Juvenile literature. [1. Crocodilians. 2. Crocodiles. 3. Alligators.] I. Title.
QL666.C9S57   1999   98-34705
597.98—dc21   CIP
                                                                  AC

Typography by Kristina Albertson
13 14 15 16 17 SCP 20 19 18 17 16 15 14 13 12 11
❖
Visit us on the World Wide Web!
www.harperchildrens.com